Learning Tree
1 2 3

Hot and Cold

By Susan Baker
Illustrated by Mike Lacey

CHERRYTREE BOOKS

Read this book and answer the questions. Ask an adult before you try any of the experiments. Heat is very dangerous. Never handle anything hot or frozen – ice can 'burn' you as well as flames.

Ask an adult or an older friend to help you with the experiments and tell you if your answers are right. Ask for help if you find the questions difficult. Often there is more than one answer to a question.

A Cherrytree Book

Designed and produced by
A S Publishing

First published 1991
by Cherrytree Press Ltd
a subsidiary of
The Chivers Company Ltd
Windsor Bridge Road
Bath, Avon BA2 3AX

British Library Cataloguing in Publication Data
Baker Susan *1942-*
Hot and Cold
1. Temperature
I. Title II. Lacey, Mike *1930-* III. Series
536

ISBN 0-7451-5151-5

Printed and bound in Italy by L.E.G.O. s.p.a., Vicenza

Does the sun make you feel hot?
What makes you feel cold?
How can you warm yourself up?
How do you cool down?

Why is this boy wearing such light clothes?

Why is this girl wearing such heavy clothes?

Why has this bear got such thick fur?

Why is this elephant spraying itself?

Which clothes do you wear in summer?
Which do you wear in winter?

What do you do if your hands are cold?
Rub them together to make them warm.
When you rub anything it gets hotter.
Rub your hand on this book and feel the heat.

Your body needs heat.
When you move you make heat.
Running about makes you feel hot.
The faster you move the hotter you get.

Everything in the world is made of tiny particles called molecules.
You cannot see them but they are always moving.
The hotter they are the faster they move.

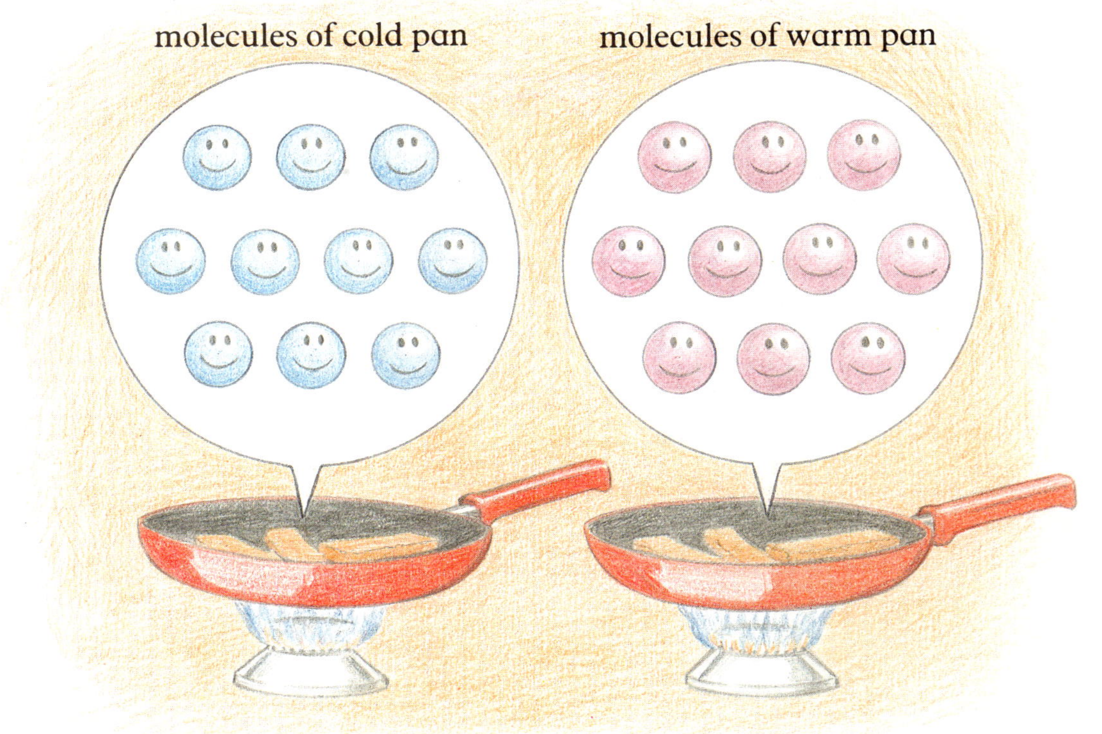

When you put a pan on the stove the molecules at the bottom move backwards and forwards.

They bump into the molecules next
to them.
Bump, bump, bump!
The pan gets hotter and hotter as they bump.

When things get really hot they burst into flames.

When you boil water it turns to steam.
The molecules move so far apart that they fly away from the water.
They turn to gas and disappear into the air.

When you cool water the molecules move together.
In the end they stick together and make ice.
The water freezes.

We all need heat to live.
We get heat from our food.
We call the heat we make energy.

We make heat by burning fuel.
Cars have to burn fuel before they can move.
We have to burn our food before we can move.

Things cannot burn without a gas from the air called oxygen.
This candle soon goes out when the jar is covered. It uses up all the oxygen.

We breathe in oxygen from the air.
We use it to burn the food we eat.
The burning of our food gives us energy.

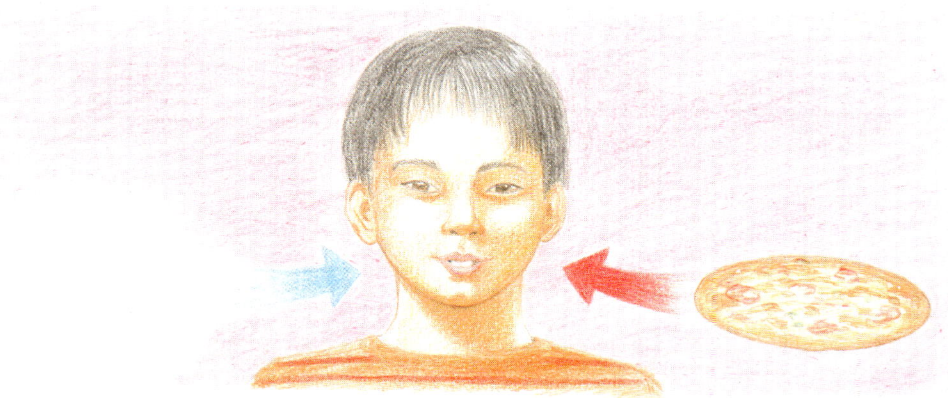

Water changes to steam when you heat it.
See how other things change when you heat them.
Get an adult to help you to test some things.

Even metal and rocks melt if they get hot enough.

See how things change when you cool them.
A jelly sets. Water turns to ice.
Test some things in your fridge or freezer.

Ice is lighter than water.
Make some ice cubes and watch them float.

Collect some things made of different materials.
Which ones feel warm? Which ones feel cool?
Do the smooth things feel warmer than the rough?
Does it matter what colour things are?

Fill all sorts of containers with hot tap water.
Leave them to cool for ten minutes.
How hot do they feel now?
Put them in order of hotness.

The hotness or coldness of something is called its temperature.
We use a thermometer to measure temperature.

You need to heat the oven to the right temperature before you bake a cake.

You need to keep your plants at the right temperature to keep them alive.

Sometimes when you are ill, you get a high temperature.
You feel hot and sweaty.

Can you tell the temperature of water?
Put one hand in cold water and one hand in hot water – not too hot.
Then put both hands in warm water.
Does the water feel hot or cold?

More about hot and cold

Good and bad conductors

Heat passes easily through some materials. Cooks use metal pans because heat from the hob travels quickly through the metal to the food. If the handle of the pan is also metal, it will heat up too. The cook has to hold it with a glove.

Most pans have wooden handles. Heat does not travel easily through wood. Metal is a good *conductor* of heat, wood is a bad one. So is plastic.

Saving heat

To keep things hot, we *insulate* them with bad conductors of heat. Air is a bad conductor – so long as it cannot move. Knitted clothes keep us warm because air is trapped by the wool. Double-glazed windows keep heat in a room because a layer of air is trapped between two panes of glass. We cover hot-water cylinders with thick fibre jackets to stop them losing heat.

We insulate things to stop them burning us. Oven doors and pan handles are made of good insulators.

Friction

When two things are rubbed together they make heat by *friction*. Long ago people started fires by rubbing two dry sticks together until the wood was hot enough to catch fire.

If you rub two pieces of ice together, they make enough heat to melt the ice. If you hammer a piece of metal the friction will make it hot.

Heat expansion

When you heat metal it gets larger, or *expands*. If a nut and bolt are hot they may be too tight to undo. If you leave them to cool, the metal shrinks, or *contracts*. It makes the nut looser and easier to undo.

Killing germs

Heating food until it is really hot makes it safer to eat. The heat kills any germs that are in the food. Freezing food also keeps it safe. At very low temperatures germs cannot breed and make food go bad.

1

1 Is it hotter at night or during the day ?

2 Why is it cold when it is cloudy?

3 Which would you prefer to eat on a cold day, a hot sausage or an ice lolly?

4 Why do you rub your hands when they are cold?

5 What will happen to this snowman in the sun?

2

6 What happens if you put ice-cream on hot apple pie?

7 Does moonlight make you feel warm?

8 If you were feeling cold and you had nothing warm to put on, what would you do: sit still or run about?

9 What is oxygen?

10 Put a night light into a small jar and get an adult to light it for you. Watch it burn for a while. Then cover the jar and watch the flame. What happens to it? Why?

11 Can you live without oxygen? Can you live without food? What do our bodies use oxygen for?

12 What happens to water when you heat it?

3

13 Make a science notebook. Write the answers to these questions in it and any more questions that you want to ask. If you notice something about heat or cold, write it down.

14 Are the molecules in ice close together or far apart?

15 If you had to sit outside on a cold day, what would you like the seat to be made of: metal, stone, wood or cloth?

16 Why are teddy bears more cuddly than dolls?

17 Why are radiators made of metal?

18 Find out what *convection* means. Why does hot air rise?

19 Find out what happens when glass is heated?

20 Fire fighters sometimes put out fires with blankets or with thick foam. Do you know why?

21 Find out about temperature scales. At what temperature does water boil on the Celsius, or Centigrade, scale? What is the same temperature in the Fahrenheit scale? At what temperature does water freeze?

22 What happens in the garden when the temperature drops below zero (0 degrees Centigrade)?

23 What should your body temperature be if you are healthy?

24 Find ten things in your house that are insulated to keep them at the right temperature.

25 If you rub two pieces of ice together, what happens to them?

Index

air 13, 21
baking 18
bear 4
body 7, 22
body temperature 19, 23
boiling water 10
breathing 13
burning 12, 13, 22
candle 13
cars 12
Celsius scale 23
Centigrade scale 23
clothes 4, 5, 21
colour 16
conductors 21
contraction 21
convection 23
cooling 3, 15, 16, 17
cool things 16
double-glazed windows 21
eating 22
elephant 4
energy 12, 13
expansion 21
Fahrenheit scale 23
fire 21
fire fighters 23
flames 9, 22
floating 15
food 123, 13, 21
freezer 15
freezing 11, 15, 21, 23
friction 21
fridge 15
frozen water 11, 15
fuel 12
fur 4, 16
gas 13
germs 21
heat from food 12
heating 8, 9, 14, 22, 23
high temperature 19
hot air 23
hot-water cylinder 21
ice 11, 15, 21, 23
insulators 21, 23
jelly 15
living 12
making heat 6, 7
melting 14
metal 14, 21, 23
molecules 8, 9, 10, 11, 23
moonlight 22
moving 7, 8
night 22
notebook 23
oven 18, 21
oxygen 13, 22
pan on stove 8, 9, 21
plants 19
plastic 21
questions 22, 23
radiators 23
rocks 14
rough things 16
rubbing 6, 21, 22, 23
running 7
smooth things 16
snowman 22
steam 10, 14
summer 5
sun 3, 22
teddy bears 23
temperature 18, 19, 20, 21, 23
thermometer 18
warming up 3, 6, 22
warm things 16
water 10, 11, 14, 15, 20
winter 5
wood 21
wool 21
zero temperature 23